EBONY
CREOLE
WHISPERS

An' Sestrel EVOLUTION OF
LOUISIANA BLACK CREOLE POETS

AmdePoet
Anthony (Amde) Hamilton

♫

Classic Cut Musiz paperback and hardcover edition
published November 2021

Los Angeles, California

United States Library of Congress Control Number:
2021948913

♫

Dedication

I dedicate this work first to the memory of my wonderful soulmate of 58 years, Sarah my love. Without her, this would not exist. Second, I dedicate this to our children, grandchildren, and great great-grandchildren. We have many. I asked all of them for generations to come, to please read your Papa's poetic thoughts, I pray that these slices of my life are of some value to you all. I am just a poet; I cannot ask others to take their precious time to read my humble verse. But I think I have a divine right as a great, great, great-grandfather to ask that my children read this one.

Love love love, *Papa*
A Watts Prophet

Table of Contents

Forward

He talks, whispers loudly on notepads, one word at a time, as does he rhyme. Exploring history as he lived it. Whispering truths, lies, greed, and most importantly the need for honesty, like his book *From Dope Fiend to Priest*. Father Amde has experienced everything in between. Congo Square is in his DNA, ancestral lineage from a New Orleans moonlit second-line dance.

There is a feeling that explores an intention when writing. Yes, I said writing, not typing. As I was blessed to have touched the manuscript, words handwritten from the 1960s to the 2020s, forward into the future.

My breath had become still, as Momma Shirley blessed the moments shared in front of the redwood estate, nestled on green, fluffy acres, quiet and cozy during the lift of a pandemic quarantine mandate.

He shared with me the intent behind the feeling of what some may call a misspelled word (italicized throughout the manuscript), even writing in pencil, those words were not erased or replaced; spirit intended them to be that way, over and over again.

So, no, they were not mistakes, because they kept coming out that way. They are spelled with a twang -some people sing, some people sang, and they both became a way of being.

I write spiritual writings; I write what the ancestors tell me. I was programed to be who I am, a Creole poet, by my grandmothers and my family, who were breeding militant poets, they put that spirit in me. This is what he shared as he addressed a group of anxious workshop attendees that eagerly listened and learned on a Watts Writers Workshop virtual meeting.

Father Amde continues to teach, reach, and whisper nuggets of wisdom to all who will receive them. His work is thought provoking, reflective, and has a timeless energy. This manuscript, in particular, celebrates the sacred Creole lineage of language, sound, and rhythm. Father Amde honors this thread and has traced it back to the earliest of people who walked the earth.

I encourage you to get your favorite cup of tea, gather your precious family, treasure every breath as you read, and share the timeless writing with your loved ones. Welcome the little ones and vibrate in Father Amde's brilliant inscriptions.

Melanie Luja
StillWaters Network

♫

Introduction

One day, some black linguists, psychiatrists, and psychologists got together and named this ever-evolving language Ebonics, meaning black sound. It continued to grow till it touched the whole earth, and at one time it was dominant in many forms of music. This sound continues to evolve. For example, in my generation we called a house a crib. Some generations called it a pad. This generation calls it a spot. I don't know what the youngsters of today are calling it, though I know that it's still evolving.

This is where The Watts Prophets came in Richard Dedeaux and I, two Creole boys who brought our artwork together at The Watts Writers Workshop. Richard and I were raised in the same culture and tradition. We ate the same kinds of food, we listened to the same kind of music, and both of us seemed to be set aside for something special in our Creole families. Each of us were trained for something.

The first poem I ever wrote was entitled Papa, and many years later I began to realize that I was trained by my papa and my grandmother to be what I am today, a poet.

My wonderful, hardworking mother had three children. She would go to work and leave us at the babysitter. My grandmother and grandfather would come and get me and leave the rest of the children. This caused a lot of tension between my mother and grandparents, yet they would insist that my mother calm down and allow them to take me. They knew they had to do something with me. So everywhere they went, I would go too. My papa was a very wise man who spoke French, my grandmother spoke Creole, they did not speak very good English. My grandmother was a seamstress and business lady, Papa could do anything except read and write.

Richard was going through some of the same things, we were going to Catholic Schools, we were both expected to marry a lil' yellow girl, and have our lil' yellow babies, and just keep it like this. However, what people didn't know about the Creole, is that he suffered, because it's terrible to be in the middle. The black people did not want you, and the white people did not want you, so that's why Creoles stuck to themselves, chose excellence, and did their own thing.

Creoles were the first in America to have a daily African American newspaper. They were the first in America to put together a black anthology on black poets. They were also some of the first African Americans to push for the vote after the civil war.

Then they literally began to breed militant poets. That's the word they used, militant.

I recall before my grandmother died, she said to me, You are the only one that took my lessons and really learned them. She also said, you learned to do two things that I'm very proud of, and that's put your foot down and speak up!, to her, put your foot down meant you are not going any further, you are going to stop and speak for yourself, and if you're pushing me, you're gonna stop, because I'm stopping it, and I'm gonna speak up! That's what I learned.

Richard Dedeaux came from that same training. His mother was also a writer. One day, I was with Richard at one of his gatherings, it was one of his elder auntie's birthdays. We were all in the garage smoking weed when his auntie came in furious because everyone was smoking weed. She told everybody to get out!, but Richard, she said, needed it for his work. She was saying he needed this herb to finish whatever work he was doing.

Richard was the master writer out of all of us. In his last interview, he mentioned that he wrote straight for forty years and nobody ever noticed him, he's never been published, he has twenty or thirty short stories, movie scripts, plays, and novels. A very brilliant cat that was very quiet about it, very subtle. However, our upbringing was in the same culture, tradition, and history, we ate the same foods and knew the same people because we were in the Creole community. To make a long story short, what I've realized is that we were bread to be these militant poets that came out of the 1960's with a name called the Watts Prophets.

I still remember a time that we (The Watts Prophets) were invited to New Orleans to present at the Essence Festival, and we were also invited to St. Augustine Church, the oldest African American Church in Louisiana. This church was built by Creoles, freed slaves, and African Americans with their own money. We were invited to a Mass at the church and allowed to get on the altar and do our poetry. (We thought, WOW!) My cousin named Yo was still a member of the church at this time, and she came to visit when we performed. My family had always been members of this church.

Richard and I were bred to be who we are. Our ancestors turned in their graves and hollered hallelujah that day we first performed, because that's what they were trying to breed: militant poets! What makes it so significant when I say the word *militant* is that was the word that was used against us in the 1960's. All you had to do is say They're militant. We would lose jobs, gates would close, etc., that one word did so much damage to our careers as artists, we were always under FBI surveillance.

In hindsight, now I understand that's what Grandma and them bred us to be: militant poets. As faith would have it, Richard Dedeaux and I somehow spiritually hooked up, I was with him when he passed. We were brothers until he transitioned. That's a slice of how we hooked into Ebonics, listening to the ebony sounds of our grandparents and ancestors.

- Amdepoet

♫

Amde's Oral Breath Mark-❯™

Poetry is an oral tradition, sound-waves that can be measured for energy and intent. The sounds of poetry are equivalent to musical notes, allowing the reader to experience the rhythm and swing of an oral composition.

This led Amde to the development of the coined Oral Musical Breath Mark alongside his brilliant grandson Gabriel, which is the new symbol used throughout this manuscript. It directs the performer of the oral passage to take a breath or to make a slight pause. Amde's creative use of the Oral Musical Breath Mark, is a new method of editing oral tradition.

♫ *Prophets come to tear down lies and build up truth*

♫

In Defense of Reality

Nothing more real than real can replace real is
reality❜ nothing added or
                    subtracted independent of
perception only real is real is real❜

Humanity must never abandon the divine sacred
value of reality❜ if I poet stand
                    alone against the world in defense of
reality with only the power
                              of poetic words
against absurd❜

I stand in eternal defense of reality forever screaming
my humble verse into the
                    universe❜ declaring my Love Love
Love of reality Not virtual
                              Reality❜ Reality❜
nothing added subtracted

multiplied or divided

        I stand in eternal defense of Reality

Google Told Me A Lie

I don't know why google told me a lie❩
  whoever or whatever google be be *lying*
sometimes with bias raciest opinions❩ Google this
google that How you know that's a fact?❩
     Google don't respect truth or lie
what you think and why that's how google get by❩

Most think google is a Scientific Expert on
everything❩ Google can make a fool
  thank they cool downloading google opinions
(creating google minds on google time)❩ (Googling
this Googling that Google motives Google
    facts)❩

Google will tell you this❩ then tell me that about a
fact what's with that?❩ Google be *lying* sometimes
and people be going goo goo ga ga ga ga ga over
   Google be *lying* sometimes to
downloaded Google minds❩ what's with that?
Googles not the Most High sometimes Google tell a
lie
     can you Google why?❩
Google be...
   be *lying* sometimes
    can you Google why?
google told me a lie❩ Echo (background voices)

Google be *lying* sometimes -repeat

♪

Algo

Selfie Selfish digital moments digital face digital taste
addicted to tech♪ Algo is standing by♪
    invisible violence in the air Algo everywhere
stealing data providing
      solutions for all institutions♪
        makes no difference where you go high
or low fast or slow Algo know♪

Algo the new spy got every tongue tapped from
Hollywood to *ghetto*
    everybody dancin' the Algo♪ most don't know
they dancin' the Algo yet it's
      the only thing they really know we all dancin'
the Algo♪ the new mentality
        created by man's virtual reality

Algo tells you what to perceive what to believe when
to laugh when to grieve♪
    downloaded minds full'a downloaded perceptions
no exceptions♪
      we all dancin' the Algo to non-organic outta
life's step in Robotic Rhythm♪
        Invisible violence in the air Algo
everywhere and a downloaded app
        Multimedia Robot mentality♪ has
become the world's reality
          Virtual has become Reality
            everybody dancin' the Algo

♪

All youth should befriend a wise elder,
youth are the beginning, elders the ending,
allowing youth, if wise to see the
beginning middle and ending
In this play called life

♫

Ebony Creole Whispers

I am a human planet in orbit
    in the universe of planets that must always be the
reality in me❩
       I have no desire
    to ever be the satellite of others realities❩
I must always
    listen to Ancestral voices dwelling in my mind
through time❩ now I know where thoughts come
from my ancestors bring them to me with poetic
power to set
      them free❩
I am their Blues and Good News❩
    for so long I was unaware those humbling voices
were there my ego was in the way❩ not allowing me
to hear clear wise Ebony Creole Whispers in my
ears❩

Born old *soul* lead by teacher preacher within❩ what
others think hear see be
    mean little to me
I will never be the satellite of others Realities❩

I must always listen carefully to the Ancient voices
within❩ everything they went *thru* is in me to❩ I am
there poetic voice of today
    the end result of millions of years of joy and tears❩
      I am their Blues and Good News

Hidden Narcissist

Flowing through life each verbal encounter spends
precious energy
    exposing me to man's many emotions♪ up and
down like a boat in turbulent oceans♪
   demanding response I must adjust to each
encounter
words disturb peaceful meditation♪
   silence becomes my adjustment♪
        at times I face vicious ulterior motives
along with large egos disguised as sweet humble
conversation♪
       one upmanship flows from their lips nothing
hip as haters probe for flaws♪ non except flaws and
all
     nor realize my every moment in life♪ adds up
to who I am at this moment?
       in this unwanted conversation of you up me
down♪
 Aloof Silence becomes my adjustment I meant no
harm I was not competing♪
     yet only one upmanship disguised as sweet
humble conversation flows
      from their lips nothing hip♪
Aloof silence my adjustment in my search for
Human Harmony
      Words disturb peaceful meditation

Ebony

Ebony my love don't despair we were here before
number one we are the zero where the one comes
from❩
We used to rule ourselves with love my friends
that beautiful day will come again❩ our sweet
entertaining spells will turn bitter to the negative
critter❩ our
stolen songs will choke them our dances will crack
their bones❩
Their tech inventions will betray their intentions❩
Poor Peoples pain a curse in the universe creating
something much much worse❩ Mama Earth will turn
to a hearse down has up up has down Mama Earth
keeps going around and around❩
Ebony is all colors in one has no beginning or
ending
We are the zero where the one comes from❩ love
and wisdom will be back Mama Earth Spins Like
that
(Repeat)

Wounded Humanity

Sad Sad Sad state open the gate Grandmother Love
can't wait not too late♪ Earth on verge of insanity led
by sane and insane doing their thing♪ Imperfect
Wounded Humanity
 Individual mass insanity embraces Humanity
impeding perfection♪ magnifying life's struggles and
troubles
 Imperfect wounded Humanity mass insanity
 in pursuit of perfections imperfections♪
never ending battle decay always on the way order
goes in and out of order fighting for balance♪
 pass the chalice let the sweet incense
of my censer touch your
 enlightenment spirit♪ born into
Wounded Humanity
sometimes pure insanity Imperfect Wounded
Humanity♪ destroying order and
 peace cultivating mass disorder
sad sad sad
 Imperfect wounded humanity

♩

Abuna Yesehaq

I went walking with a holy Monk into unholy lands
Archbishop Yesehaq his name loving Most High
truth and righteousness his everything❩
Frankincense in air then he would appear A General
in Gods army❩ who prayed a lot for haves and have
nots

This leader of Monks was sent west by the King of
Kings to find sinners with tradition culture and
history make winners❩ Ancient Ethiopian cross in
hand he left the Holy peaceful loving protection of
the monastery❩ moving humbly into the evil cities of
the world into the valley of Godless hearts❩ most
times in pain fragile weak little sleep yet spiritually
strong he strolled deeper west into deep deep moral
mess❩

He teacher I student began my walk with this Holy
Monk from Trench Town to Watts and many other
spots he fought for haves and have nots❩
Blessings and Baptizing thousands in the West never
able to rest or go back to his beloved monastic nest❩
before those he loved and worked to save Crucified
Him❩

I will never forget walking with a Holy Monk into
unholy lands

♩

Moments

In the inner atmosphere of my mind,
sweet memory moments like sweet wine
soothes my aging mind

in tune n time, each precious
magic mystical moment
yesterday or today
become crystal clear

as time ages my soul
each moment
turns to pure gold

♫

Winter

Strolling the winter of life without the love of my life
to place a warm loving blanket
  on my gentle soul when life is cold❩
  As I stroll on alone through blizzards storms
sometimes sunny warm strolling to
    life's next good or bad mysterious step hoping
for laughter not he wept❩
      I accept joy and sorrow as same
            one end or other
                  bottom other end of top
                  Cold other end of hot❩
As I stroll on sometimes stumbling fumbling tripping
slipping until I find my
  balance and stroll on right or wrong must keep
strolling into the unknown with
    a big smile❩ mixed with extra pep in my feeble
steps strolling through winter
        of life destination unknown
              But Boldly strolling on

Freedom Tree

Allow me to tell you about a beautiful tree in a alley
that mean so much to me called Freedom Tree by
the Watts community❩

Under this large elegant tree you could learn to win
or lose you only had to choose❩ its branches reached
far and wide it had stood here *listening* a long time❩
all type of humans could be found under this tree❩
the lawyer enslaved and free all visited The Freedom
Tree

Drunks came to crash thief to steal his cash atheist
and philosopher came to understand and debate
preacher man❩ good and bad deals were made in its
shade young and old rich poor sat on its dirt floor❩
sweet singing birds came to nest and rest dogs and
cats came to eat cast away mess❩

Artist painted the scene poets screamed romance
bloomed all who came fell under the mystic spell of
this holy tree❩
In the mist of poverty and pain love flowed free
wisdom history and tradition was in air yet a fool
could be found there❩

Time stood still under the sacred leaves of this
mystic tree everyone felt free in harmony❩ young and

old learned from each other everyone became sister and brother❩

When cold winters came the atmosphere remained the same they made fire in big trash cans where preacher warmed his hands next to *liars*❩

Then one beautiful day Urban Renewal came with a claim to improve our lot cut down our freedom tree scattering the wisdom harmony and misery❩ leaving a empty lot and no shade for the have nots
        No shade for the have nots

♫

Small Things

Small things become big things in small brains
      minor become major low becomes loud
           little room left for understanding
              because small things become big things
in small brains
                  simple becomes complicated
                    a stream of emotion turns into a
turbulent ocean of emotion
                      a spark into an explosion
   No room left for understanding logic or reason in
any season
              because small things become big things in
small brains
                No room left for Understanding

♫

Poets don't need an army or gun,
they are the real army of one

Truth has trouble in the mist of lies,
but remember I and I, truth survives

Ebony politics

Civil rights leaders grab on to
  popular issue like tears to
    tissue❩ act as if they helpin'
      the poor they the only ones
get more more more poor
stay poor get what little left like a
  dog eating a leftover bone all the
meat be gone❩

Professional talkers talking that talk
 never walk the walk stumbling
  down blind alley of
    protest caught up in old
      mess instead of progress❩
        dwelling on past pain
          instead of doing a
new thing while cherishing history but moving on❩
weak politicians grab on to
      popular crisis issues like tears to tissue
      talking talk never
walking the walk
 just talk
 talk
talk
talk

Silence

Silence in nature allows you to hear Music in the
gentle breeze it's instruments birds bees and trees❩
Silence is a big band with multi organic rhythmic
sounds all around❩
 the roosters just crowed
    hoot hooted owl moooo the cow woodpecker
pecking tender notes in different trees played by
rhythm breeze birds and bees❩ life's silent sound
natures
      orchestra be gettin' down❩
 Silence the key
    to hear a stream sang
      a song or the emperor
        of birds the vulture
          screams in Key on
        time with hummingbirds
wings doing
they rhythmic things❩
two different notes in different trees played by the
Tender breeze woodpeckers
birds and bees
 allowing all to hear
   how LOUD SILENCE
can be

Counselor

Where does the counselor
   go for counseling?♪ who holds
      the cup for their tears
         weakness and fears?

I ask where is
     the understanding ears that
     will hear the counselor
        screaming years♪
           weakness and fears?

To a friend♪ my
     friend Krishna
        said as she with wisdom
          counseled me

♫

It ain't always what they said,
it's why they said
what they said

♫

Ms Dignity

Siting on ground in Lotus position
   in front of church on MLK Blvd.❥
      homeless with grace dignity and Elegance
all she owns neatly stacked in
       little piles surrounding her❥

Her powerful spirit penetrates my *soul* each time I
pass
   where does she go for private things or when it
rains I wondered?❥
      good or bad weather she sleeps on concrete
under cardboard on a
       blanket bed she carefully makes each
dangerous night❥
        sometimes she reading or cleaning her
nails she has not lost her
        pride nor the gentle womanly
touch that make something simple so much❥

With her beautiful multicolored head rag for a
   crown she's a Queen homeless
    sitting in the cold dirt of life with grace
elegance and dignity alone in pain

     wounded with a Smile!

Poems

Poetic souls become pregnant
with poems❥ some never leave
 mind or enter time❥ others born
are trashed or buried in coffins
   of old cast away notebooks❥ others
      have short unique lives

Then there
   are poems that leap from
      the page❥ move out on their own❥
      as they gently touch hearts
      and *souls* of mankind❥
         to live forever in the
            universal memory of no
      time in the library of
         humanities minds

♩

Creativity

Watts's flavor flowing from Jelly Roll Morton
passing thru to bass strings of Charlie Mingus
   into multi rhythm drumbeats
      of Billy Higgins♩ blending
  with Horace Tapscott's black and white
            keys♩ Avant-garde
Ornette Coleman♩ organic Don Cherry please♩
Composers of complex creativity♩
 Watts Prophets flavor eccentric
  some say♩ but in Watts we
      just do it our way!

♫

*Land is where man stand
culture is how he expand
creating history standing
on God's land*

*Old folks say a man falls in Love
first with his eyes,
a woman, her Ears*

Learning How to Love

It takes time
 to learn how to love
  it don't always fit like a hand
   in a glove nor is it sent
      from Cupid above♪

It takes patient in time to
 learn how to love♪ being
  selfish demanding
    never compromising *lying*
       conniving won't do trying to make one out of
two♪

Tender Gentle love the glue
  do me fair like I do you
    until we both see
      love don't always fit like hand in glove
         nor is it sent from Cupid above♪

It takes worktime patience
 and forgiveness to learn how to love
    Tenderly

You cannot imprison the word,
it can enter unseen anywhere
there is a mind

♩

Redwoods

Big big Redwoods sipping fog
  from clouds❭ king of trees
    trying not to become some man's
        Log

 Living antennas into the
   universe❭ loved by birds and
        bees from bottom to top

Life lives❭ tree gives❭ as it
  filters air for humanity

Everywhere sipping fog
   in the sky❭ Redwood trees❭
     Earths antennas reaching for
      the Most High

Institution Building

Institution building is
 like planting a seed it's something every nation
needs❯
It takes a man with a dream a wise scheme a team
        that must work themselves like a man that plows
Earth❯ until it's fertile and full of creative worth
   Deeds unity honesty and discipline
          are seeds they'll need to succeed❯
like a little infant tree that struggle threw
          earth to be free
              a young institution struggle to be❯
it must weather the storm of deceit
    those who would cheat to beat❯
because competitiveness sometimes
become viciousness all of this
        the one who guides the institution must miss❯
He must see way
 ahead in his head have a pioneer creative
    mind and realize that growth takes
                        hard work time❯
Deep into the earth
 like the root of a big oak tree
        an institution must claim it's turf by service
          prove it's worth❯ by doing this it will be able
    to stand the crushing changing blows of time and
like the sun in the sky
                    forever Shine

Enter-Net

I hear People Say each and every day
That the internet will set modern man free like
a dolphin in the sea❯

Now this statement completely confused me
Since when has a net set anything free❯

Now my simpleness I regret
But where's the freedom in a net

Fishermen's makes nets, spiders weave webs Botha
are traps❯
The spider knows all in his website
He keeps it in site day or night
Wrap real real tight, with a click and a byte❯

Is it online or in line
Download or unload

Where is the freedom in a net?❯

Stealth traps in you laps
Net zero hero's
Sky tell intel DSL Email

Tell
Tell
Tell❯

Processing your personal soul for info
No telling where it go
Only net maker really know♪

Now, you used to be able shred it
But know that's jive
The hard drive is always alive

Wrap real real tight with a click and a bite

Spiderman can pull you up tonight♪

Free man freely entering net
Will one day experience regret
Because there's no freedom in a net

Fishermen controls their net
Spiders control their webs
And who controls the world wide web you're in?♪
What spider have you in its website
Wrapped real real tight

♫

Positive and negative are
one when you learn to balance
them on a scale of life,
the beauty of life will embrace you
until then, your scales will be rockin'

♪

Truth

I fell in love with truth♪

  started shouting it loud with
    no finesse

Putting truth to test
  got me in a lot of mess

Blunt truth can be
  a strong distasteful overdose for most♪
    except in a poetic toast

♪

Monks Say

Tears are the blood of a
    bleeding heart
 Much respect in prayer
 by the Gods

♩

Oppression of human evolution
cultivates and breeds revolution

♫

Faith

Don't put yourself in the dark
a person who walks by faith
not sight is blind faith
and sight both gifts of the
Creator so keep your
eyes open in dark or
miss the light when
it appears

Giving

I spent my life giving a hand
  to woman or man did not give to get
    knowing how quick we forget♪

        Knowledge say you reap what
        you sow Life showed me that
          ain't the way it always go♪
              you can sow positive
                reap negative like
                  sowing a smile
                  and reaping a
                      Frown

♫

The blues will take you
under if you don't learn to swing it

Most time the fruit
don't taste like the root,
sometimes the root
is more tasty than the fruit,
you can have a Bitterroot with
sweet fruit, or bitter fruit with Sweet Roots

♫

Thoughts

No one knows where thoughts come from
   not wise to except everyone
         thoughts come and go
You have the power to keep or let go
            win or lose because of thoughts you choose
Beautiful thoughts
               becomes beautiful things
                  ugly thoughts
                     ugly things
positive thoughts positive things
                  because thoughts are
                                    things

♩

Friendship

(Friendship needs cultivation and constant
    Protection) must never appear shady♪

    Friendship
      is an ear when no other
        hears your tears and fears♪ lose
          or win they stick in a handkerchief
            to dry your tears will tell you truth
            you don't
              want to hear♪ see
                detail become a soft
                  pillow for a bruised
                    head♪
      Always
        deep never shallow a crutch
          when life is too much♪
        cheer you on till you get where
        you' goin'

      Trust
        must Never be in question
          True friendship needs
            Protection

♩

No Work for Poet today

No work for Poet today hidden
            hands in the way of truth Poets
                              must say❩
Social comments not welcome
      crime of opinion enforced by
                              thought police❩

Poets always outta time not toeing
   apt line often politically in correct❩

No work for Poet today the world
         wants book sellers
                  not truth tellers❩

Hidden hands mold opinions
      central control politics and gold
              no work for Poets today❩ Poets
                      want to save their *souls*

No work for Poet today freedom of speech
   something we teach
                  not reach

No work for Poet today

♩

*The shepherd saves the sheep
from the wolf, so he can eat them!*

*My heart was always in the
right place, when I knew
what the right place was*

♩

Pray

I don't pray much anymore
   I know the Lord has an overload
     of serious request because
       man is taught to pray nonstop
        for their needs and desires❥

              I decided to leave room for those who
                          need it
                       most

              The creator has always been good to me❥
       so I will allow our Lord some needed rest
from my mess
      by making my every
           Action a Prayer not requiring Words

Family Secrets

Family secrets hide in dark or light
can be wrong or right dull or bright♪
secrets pass from kin to kin
to next Generation

Truth or lie family secrets don't die♪
poison secrets move on and on
Family mess never put to rest♪
secrets nobody let die
open and close eyes dark light
dull bright wrong or right
poison secrets fail to die♪

Families pass them on keeping dead
alive hiding poison secrets
in shallow minds♪
Family secrets live on
right or wrong hiding
in dark or light
wrong or right

Family mess never put to rest

In and out Memories

All humans are in and out world only see what in
   lets out❩ Gaze deep into my blood shot eyes and
      see what in let out of me

   Life pictures my minds eyes have taken in time
      placed in the memory album of my mind❩
   Memories blurred others clear
   some far others near déjà vu anytime is a stroll
thru the colorful pictures in my mind❩

Frozen Memories New Orleans Texas LA Mama
Papa Gran'Ma Uncle Baba Aunt Nanee Fast Black
Okey Doke three Popes❩ strolled
Egypt's desert on this less traveled road❩ of
   warm cold vivid memories

People good bad happy sad pain loss gain sweet
      bitter a baby a litter home car a
         critter❩ Empty frames no names
      Brilliant cats in Borsalino hats in Cadillacs❩

Permanent fixtures pictures that can be seen deep
within my blood shot eyes memories blurred some
clear far or near some gone some still Here❩
People be in and out
         World only see what In let Out

♪

Today

Today is in the way
　　　　of yesterday

People who can't
　　　　　　　see ahead I show hate to see
today❩
they take progress back
　　　　talking about past pain
　　　　　　　　old game
　　　　　　　ain't that
　　　　　　　a shame❩
I'm doing my day today
　　on my way to tomorrow
　　　　you can't use a dollar
　　　　spent last week but
　　　　　　you can make one
　　　　　　　　today to spend
　　　　　　　　　tomorrow

Double Minded

Man can't be double minded
    if in life he wants to find it
        looking to ways with one set of eyes
                will confuse a wise guy♪
One can't be good and bad too that's
    one cut in two not a together you
      a double mine stays
        confused all the time
          will two types of fruit
            grow on one vine?♪
Don't lose out at the fork of your life
    choose a trail that leads from hell
        here on earth♪ preserving your *soul*
          for a new birth beyond earth
Man can't go but one way doing
        a day
          a day
            getting closer to the
              end and birth again
                with no END♪
Will your spirit go
through life grabbing onto strife?
        or will it gather good and nice?
          some advice♪
Virtue or vice
    Universal truth is light
        allowing man to see his path
   in Darkest of Night

Ebony Babies Eyes

She was peeping *through* the plate glass window of
Uhuru in her brown eyes so young I could see "Mr."
What must I do?❯
My mouth is bloody
       my clothes muddy three demons have me
           in their sick non-feeling ghetto net❯
They want to do something in life I shall always
regret but being ghetto rats rape to them not regret❯
not even my life if they took would they regret❯
My mind is drugged from ghetto pain a life of angel
dust and devil red I thought would be a better bed
      but now Sir I seem dead with a clogged
          stagnant head❯
My dad he's not bad but works so hard he's always
tired for me he has little time for him he drinks wine
to keep his mind❯
MaMa's good but thinks I'm a hood always watches
TV with her mind for the thirteen of us she has no
time❯
    I must talk to someone before I lose my mind
      Mr. could you help me please? is what I saw in
Ebony Babies Eyes❯
As tears flowed on my heart a heavy load
    I thought with action and rescued her from these
demons something in her was deep in me
      I was so happy I could
set her free

Hip-Hop World

Hip-hop world don't be fooled there's no old and
new school
Birth makes you a lifelong student of one school the
school of life❯

Fresh fruit on a tree would never look down at its
roots and say old school roots Seed root and fruit are
one❯ Root nourish fruit
Can't be no fruit without root stronger the root
greater the fruit complete expression of seed in root
is fruit❯

Being human you can change your taste in this space
but not your family root base❯ your ancestors are the
other end of you that don't mean you do what they
do you do you❯ but they still the other end of you
you can't get away from your DNA

So don't be fooled there is no old and new school❯
the same stream of blood flows from generation to
generation
the human building blocks of a great nation❯

Cultivate love unity rust and understanding among
each other
don't be fooled there is no old and new school

Seed Root and Fruit are One

♪

Nothing in life belongs to you,
not even life If it was yours,
you would never give it up

Because something is valuable
does not mean you value it
Man must value each other,
then put value on the valuable

Breed What You Need

An Elder man told me children today
  are Raised like chickens- thrown into the world to
grow not knowing what they need to know or which
way to go❯
  Son he said Lend me your ear and I will make it
clear! Planting seeds in the garden of young brains is
a deep deep thing❯ You've got to breed what you
need or evil will plant its seed❯
  Man is fertile like Earth what seeds are planted
determine his worth❯ the cultivation of your child's
mind must be done on your time
a chicken don't let a duck raise its chicks
  making chickens act like ducks❯ Man must
   protect and educate the fruit of his own
    vine or leave a generation blind❯
Fish run in fish schools and learn fish rules
  ducks quack roosters crow- a fact we all must
know❯ copycat is a fact when it comes to
  things like that❯ When a man sows his seeds he
can be sure he ain't getting weeds❯ Plant God first
     deep into the soul of a new birth
throw righteous seeds where you see a need
  plant respect and that expect❯
  Sprinkle the seed of faith love love love and
   work early in the garden of a young child's
    mind❯ and divineness shall occupy
    their time
      You've got to breed what you need!

♫

Head Rag for a Crown

She has wisdom to pass around wears a head rag
for a Crown Big momma some say is her name
Grandma Grandmother or Na Na others claim♪

From the throne of ol' rocking chair raw
season vibes of life flow into the air♪ she's a scout of
life who has looked ahead allowing sweet mother
wisdom to settle in the bedroom of her head♪

With her head rag for a Crown she carries
her heavy load down life's dusty rusty bumpy road
with an artistic taste a solid moral base♪
queen of elegance and grace deep streams of
beauty flow through her gentle face

Mother of old man river spirit giver♪
she has wisdom and knowledge to pass around
she wears a head rag for a Crown♪

A wise eyed understanding one that
rises with the sun a kind stern smooth
humble word for everyone♪ always spicy meat for
her grandchildren to eat while they sit on her fragile
knee and learn the history of their family tree♪

She's a God loving light a soldier in
the Army of right advising all far and near
and wise enough to hear the well-seasoned

♫

knowledge of many years⟩

Over the seasons day by day her physical being
rust away allowing her spirit to flow free into
eternity⟩

Love honor and glory in her abound she has
    wisdom to pass around
            a queen who wears a head rag for a Crown

I Met Me

I've had plenty fun shot plenty dope often thought
there was no hope
    But being a man who thought I fought and
searched for the key that would set me free
        from a hype-hustling - hard day and night♪

Out one cage into another not knowing I had a
mother Sister or Brother Heavy Felonies each and
every day never knowing when I might get blown
away taking folks' stuff away!♪

Dope dealers inflating their egos from the cries of
the damned
  Let me go short this time man!
    Take my coat my hat see anything else you want
let me know Jack
        I'm trying to put another mark in this track♪

Scheming and treacherous - watch me when I come
around! I'll do anything to get down!♪
  Sick days in so many ways reasons crashed from
so much Pain! It's a miracle I didn't go insane
  Searching
    Searching
      Searching
        for a way to get away

To God I went and fell to my knees in confused
sincerity❩ I begged God God God!
 Show me the path that leads away from addiction❩

Over and over I begged the Lord to give me a hand -
disillusioned hurt and still hooked
    I dug deeper into the Little Black Book❩ and
continued on
Searching
  Searching
    Searching

Then one God-sent day I met me❩ and we started to
talk I told me not to play games - it was not
    necessary us being the same❩ deep within each
other we went
      weakness I found so me began to plant fresh
and new seeds and pull the weeds❩

I taught me patience courage the art of thanking Me
showed I the way to
      Wisdom Knowledge and Understanding
                            Now I'm free
                        I'm
                          Sho' glad
                            I met ME!

♫

PAPA

Papa used to say something wise to me
each day take life seriously always son
respect everyone❩

Make your word your Bond it's the sum of you
and what you do if you say it mean it
screen it if it's dirty
clean it❩ see clearly that you mean it

A lie my boy is like a fly
now it's here there looking for a place to die❩

Truth has proof
like it be a hole when you pull a tooth

Fat meat is greasy
living right ain't easy❩ those are facts clearly
Seen unless man is living a dream❩

First was the Word so a no-good word
is absurd It's a key to the unreal a bad deal
that locks up truth in a cage of lies
attacks facts with open eyes❩

So be solid son stick love and truth
to everyone
        Papa used to say something wise to me each day

Struggling With Spirit

What should I do? I asked my Spirit
practice divine love tell truth be truth♩ or should I
enter the vicious game of life a lie?♩
If I tell truth be truth nothing worldly will I have
which is of more value to me truth?
    A pretty roof?
      A gold tooth?
        A slick car?
          A war?♩

Spirit you say be Godly♩ but in this world I see
hardly any Godly
  life on earth so short I say why must I not be able
to enjoy all that be here today?♩
 I am Spirit this I say: there is nothing today of more
value than a Godly way♩

Know you and you will know that divine love
wisdom
  knowledge and understanding♩ mixed with truth is
far above material love♩
Tune in to the Universe converse with nature life
here merely part brotherhood
    is love a forever thing stuck to the heart and brain
      of all that are righteous in life♩

♫

Clear your head come alive take care of your body
on Earth be wise use truth for proof and
    see clearly eternity within thee❩
Life on earth has some meaning Spirit I say I can
think of many beautiful things to do today
 like a love affair with a Ebony Zulu Queen❩ or
getting high
   digging life go by checking twinkle in baby's eye❩
   Now tell me why I can't do my thing?❩

I am spirit this I say: ain't nothing in life that ain't life
some nice some Vice❩

Man must live life according to divine nature❩
  flesh and mind must be on time in tune with
Spirit❩ he must learn of Mother Earth
    Sun Moon and Stars what part of them are him
from which grows wisdom knowledge
    and understanding❩

Flesh is a small part that comes and goes
 but the Spirit of you is everything forever all
complete
  command of Flesh and Spirit is what man must
seek Meet Your
   Holy Spirit
     and meet God!

Soothsayer Player

I just passed a little shady store
 with a sign painted on the door seven miracle
candles sold here❯

   I turned back and went in this diabolical looking
den within sitting in a chair
      was an old lady with glitter in her hair a cross
here a snake there candle light
        everywhere❯ the smell of sweet incense in the
air a skull hanging from her chair

Welcome my son she said A vision of you
 just flew through my head you see I read Man's
destiny❯

 Now tell me the amount of your donation to my
situation for the elimination of
    negative vibrations❯ demons I will even fight if the
price is right I'll talk to God for you
     there is nothing I can't do confidence in me is
assured victory❯
You see my Lord is close to me

 I have roots and herbs bats and birds master's oil
doves' blood and if you wish I'll cause a flood❯

Now tell me the amount of your donation

73

to my situation for the elimination of negative
vibrations❩ feeling as if I was in a cell
   somewhere in hell my story I began to tell I told of
my lack of money and my trouble
with my honey she slowly said with her ol' wrinkled
hand on her head❩
   that I needed a sweet love root some exotic fruit❩
a John the Conqueror root a specially dressed green
candle and some oil for the door handle❩ some get-
away powder gold dust and some other stuff❩ from
there we went to the till and I paid my very very large
bill as she slowly said with her old wrinkled
     hands on her head❩

Thank you my friend see you next Sunday at ten for
part two of what you must do
 for the elimination of negative vibrations
  Hehe
   Hee
    Heee

♫

When in fear, be wise, humble, bold, hot, warm, cool, or cold; always protect your mind, body and soul

Wisdom and Knowledge

Wisdom and Knowledge left college
   Wisdom went east to a feast
      Knowledge went north southeast and west
         In conquest♪ Technology became life's test
Wisdom hid cause of what knowledge did
hid away 'til Judgement Day♪

Knowledge moved on as far as the moon
   cracked the Earth took its worth
      stole man from life messed up air
         poison everywhere♪

Creative knowledge without wisdom flourished
bigger bombs were made and dropped on have nots
birth control became the goal♪
   knowledgeable Monsters gained control
souls were stole for mere gold technique was in the
minds of mankind♪ Floating in wine
   sailing through life in a therapeutic way learning
      new technical tricks life slowly sliding away♪

Books not feeling was life's thing Man checked
   a book on how to cook took his life to a psyche
      into a book he would look♪ to label your
brain
Schizoid Paranoid or some other Technical jive
   that make you look at you and not he♪

♫

Remember my Brothers and Sisters what I say to
you
life has showed me all this pain labeled an Evil
thing♪
    but raise your heads high cause knowledge
      without Wisdom will die

Wisdom hid 'cause of what knowledge did
Hid away 'til Judgement Day

                  And that ain't far away

♪

Without fine arts there are no fine minds

Today, I abandon hope and embraced destiny

Sweet Sweet Sweet Sarah

Sweet sweet Sarah sent from the most high
            Sweet
                        Sweet
                                    My love
                                    Sweet Sarah♪ My Love
      Spiritually strong Gentle Creative Orderly Neat
Not one to retreat straight ahead truth her thang♪
                        If you come aroun' She'll read your
brain
The most high gave her the ability to see thangs
Like Madam Laveau she know♪
Sweet
            Sweet
                        Sweet Sarah My Love
Leave a profound impression with her every
expression♪
      It's in her walk her talk her complete artistic style
brings me a loving smile child♪
 Sweet Sweet Sweet Sarah My Love♪
kind tender slender wise one who always makes me
happy
She's the best medicine I ever had
Sweet
            Sweet
                        Sweet
                                    Sarah My Love♪
Life's spiritual inspiration in life's diverse situations♪

♫

Sweet Sweet Sweet Sarah My Love Kind Tender𝄐
Gentle Slender
                              A wise one I will always remember
Sweet Sweet Sarah My love𝄐 Wise one I will always
remember
          Spiritually strong Gentle creative orderly neat
                    not one to retreat straight ahead truth her
thang𝄐
Sweet Sweet Sarah my love𝄐
   Kind tender slender a wise one I will always
remember
Sweet Sweet Sweet Sarah
 Sweet
                Sweet
                          Sweet Sarah
Mother of a large large flock Her DNA clock will
never stop
Tick
   Tock
      Tick Tock
         Tick Tock   Tick Tock
Tick Tock Tick Tock

♫

A Bump in the Road

Trouble ain't nothing but a bump in the road
   Grandma would say No matter how
     difficult the day or unclear the way❩
       trouble ain't nothing but a bump in the road
she would smile and say Go over it
  around it detour if you' not sure
    there's more than one way to make the play
      to have a good day❩ Grandma would smile
and say humming as she walked away

Sunup sundown was her workday
    struggling and scuffling her pay❩
yet she would smile and say Son to win in life
 keep a positive mind don't drink much wine
  do little crying keep on trying❩
   don't trust easy man can be sleazy

Keep your business to yourself you will gain wealth❩
 and always remember ain't a bump in the road the
  Most High courage and creativity can't get you
   through if you love and trust you❩

Because no matter how heavy the load life really ain't
nothing but a little bump on an endless road!

Grandma would smile and say humming as she
  walked away

Swinging the Blues

I'm a poet Swinging the Blues
    I break literary and social rules
       bring good and bad news from a poetic mind
          trying to rhythm with reason living in a bad
season❩
      Self-destruction is the way life is played today
        rude is in everything in decay
           It seems like man wants it that way❩

I'm a poet Swinging the Blues
  paying too much dues watching love lose
    surrounded by a callous generation in a dangerous
      toxic situation❩ lost in virtual reality thinking
      its reality hate's growing higher
        the people continue to exalt the liar!❩

I'm a Poet Swinging the Blues
    fighting back trying not to lose❩ in search of my
groove Swinging these Blues❩ life owes me
        nothing states an old cliche I don't see it that
way! Life owes me every day the Most High sends
my way man must learn to love each other
                      Until that day❩

I'll be Swinging the Blues breaking
  literary and social rules bringing good and bad
    news Swinging the Blues

Poetic Thoughts

Some folks talk so good
they talk themselves right outta' right

Bashfulness Unawareness Humility Divineness
Kind gestures from the Heart will get a Heart

A strong leader with a weak idea is
            A danger to life

Less you say less your tongue gets in your way

When you block Evolution
            You get Revolution

A person who will
            do anything
            anything can happen

Love on a Bus Stop Bench

She was sitting
  on his lap on a bus
    stop bench where they
      had spent their homeless
        night hugged up real tight♪
They smelled foul from
  the need of a bath
    their hair was dirty uncombed
      matted and tangled
        He had on a ragged trench coat
She had on the lining♪ but the amazing
  thing to me they were
    both smiling♪
      He caressed her gently
        on his lap with pride
Their poverty they could
  not hide♪ he kissed her
    cheek real gentle and sweet
      she smiled love♪ squeezed him tight
        With all her might
          For All to see who passed like me
            they were in love on a Bus Stop Bench
They had overcome cold poverty Hunger
and pain and made
              Love they thang

The 'Po Can't Take No Mo'

There is something I'd like the whole wild world
to know that is the po' can't take no mo'❩

The rich is going to have to open equalities golden
doors
or the poor is gon' to kick him to the floor

because like I said before the po' they can't take no
mo'❩

Now old billionaire he swear he's fair
but his logic don't hold no air there's war hunger
pain and suffering everywhere❩

For some rent so high their roof is the sky as
astronauts fly by in multi-billion-dollar toy machines
made of po' peoples hopes and dreams
it makes me want to scream❩

The po' they can't take no mo'

The rich is going to have to open equalities golden
doors
Or the poor like I said before is gonna kick them to
the floor

Because like I said before the po' they can't take
     no mo'!

Pain

Pain
  Pain
    Pain
A little for some and a whole lot for others
 complete crushing for those who don't understand
that in this society
pain is a major part of man♪ Endure you must or be
crushed

Pain
  Pain
    Pain
Like fire in the eyes burning flesh leave me sane♪ do
not mix my
mind and leave me blind

The Pain of a disease that has no cure the pain of
 a love affair that got nowhere the pain of a system
where oppression you bear♪

The pain of a war that has no end cruel people that
inflict
Pain
  Pain
    Pain
for monetary gain♪

The pain that a man has to endure when junior flip
corrupt police
put him in the position where he must choose against
humiliation as a man
 or death!♪
Pain
     Pain
         Pain
like busting babies' heads against cement walls

The Pain Pain Pain of people going to the moon
    while children in the ghettos of the world hustle
        hard day and night trying to eat♪

Hand me down hats♪ hand me down shoes
  everything used used pain and they want to know
why we don't follow rules♪

There are two little brothers that I know who
    someday would like to go to dinner an' a show
       Yea just a plain old show♪ How much did you
say that last moon-shot cost? Leave yo' head
   cause you oughta be dead
 Pain
     Pain
        Pain

A little for some and a whole lot for others

♫

Poetic Thoughts

There's a continuity in thought and principle that
continues to surface throughout my work
    Whether it's a poem quote or some poetic
thoughts this vibration is a constant
        It will show-up and insert itself wherever it
sees fit My obedience to this energy is the reason one
might find some of my earlier work nestled in the
pages of my latest work
As stated before A poets life becomes a poem

        Positive and negative are one when
you learn to balance them on a scale of
life
        the beauty of life will
embrace you
        until then
your scales will be rockin'

Poetic Lines Flowing through My Mind

Never stir strife it endangers peace limb and life

Life today a job that needs a job to survive

Fool with a fool and you will get some Foolishness

A decision must have protection if in it you want perfection

Change with time or be last in line

Google is knowledge without Wisdom

Technology indoctrinates your children without your permission

Hidden fears breed hidden tears

What is life without a hug

Some Say Some do which one are you?

Minor voices playing major parts fail before they start

If first was the word second was the lie

Everything comes in seasons not till it's ripe can you take a bite?

America murders its Elders it has no culture to caress them

In life always know your way out before you go in

Day won't come till you finish with night

Words can make an idiot sound intelligent or the insane sound sane

Youth elders are trying to slow down to catch-up with ya'll!

Technology is not neutral it embodies the desires of its creator

A beautiful Rose without a sweet smell is an injured Rose

All youth should befriend a wise
elder
Youth are the beginning
Elders the ending allowing youth if
wise to see the beginning middle
and the ending
In this play called life

I don't believe man is created
in the image of God - God is
perfect I thought man is
not I know!

The European man says we
Africans were the most superstitious
people on earth never realizing we were reading
the wisdom and spirit of the universe their eyes
could only see knowledge

Poetic Lines Flowing through My Mind

Stealing and lying are sisters and brothers

Stress is no way out knowing there is a way
out Secrets of life come to life

Death is the Apex of love Man's greatest
wealth Good Health

Cherish history always But move on
Nature has become a little park you pay to
see called Yosemite

Wisdom comical or absurd a word is just a
word

Living too slow is the same as living too fast
you still end up last

Life is a bunch of chores you must keep up
with

Life is about living sometimes giving not
getting

Truth don't belong to anyone Truth belongs
to truth

Cursing curses the one cursing that's why it's
called cursing

♫

We no longer listen to the music of life
unless it comes from an electronic device

♩

I thank God for blessing
me with a Queen for a wife
who help me survive this
sweet and bitter poetic
Life

I have met so many people
who know everything yet
can't change a thing
I pray
all those illuminated minds
remember to much light
can blind

Master teachers whose
students continue to fail
are they really Master
Teachers?

♪

Prisoner's advice to a prisoner
use your own mind
do your own time
walk slow and drink
plenty water

Most time the fruit
don't taste like the root
Sometimes the root is
more tasty
than the fruit
You can have a Bitterroot
with sweet fruit
or a bitter fruit with
Sweet Roots

♩

GrandMa say, "Make do is what
you do until you get thru"
 Make do means do what you
 have to do to get thru
 find comfortable in
 uncomfortable

Humans must learn to choose
their emotions not let their
emotions
choose them Emotions appear
in the mind no one knows where
thoughts come from you can
accept
or reject any thoughts or emotion

♫

I am always told to edit my
 work I have bad grammar they say
  To the editors of the world I ask
   what is the grammatically
correct way to scream?
   the essence of my work
sometimes a
              painful
                    scream

Poetic Lines Flowing through My Mind

A parable is a motivator into in-depth
creative thought

Love is action not just a word a verb anything
less is Absurd

Impossible to go nowhere you will always end
up somewhere

A green bush turns brown hold onto life until
it's last Greenleaf

Poetry is a deep dip into the well of one's
heart we're feelings start

I wonder why people waste my time asking
my advice when they have already taken their
own

Someone or something may cause your
madness but it is your madness that destroys
you

Men can be good in a instant evil

When you see me stumbling around know
that I'm drunk from Poetic lines intoxicating
my mind

♫

A little pretty singing bird visited me today
flew away before I could understand what it
was trying to say

Life is not fair or unfair it is life only man is
fair or unfair and that's life

♪

*Grandma Taught me when it comes to
defending right day or night put your
foot down and speak up!*

*People say it's always darkest
before day
I sure hope it works out that
way it's real dark today*

*I find peace within but it's not enough
standing in a storm will disturb
the deepest of peace
People with no ambition are out
of today's tradition they seek
peace the rest seek a piece!*

*In the inner atmosphere of my mind
sweet memory moments like sweet wine
so-izz' my aging mind in tune
in time each precious magic
mystical moment yesterday
or today become crystal
clear as time ages my
soul each moment turns
to pure gold*

♩

Life is an illusion that
comes to a conclusion in
time only ideas survive
the conclusion

The reception of good advice not
always nice some here half or
none of what's said nothing
settles in their head sometimes
those who hear it all label
you a know it all

I'm a poet
moving *through* treacherous
life with only two friends
God and my Wife

Respect Wisdom or it will be your
downfall

Poetic Lines Flowing through My Mind

I forgot to be happy today I must stop doing
that happiness is a choice I can except or
reject

Safeway store ain't safe no mo' everywhere
you go in the sto' there's GMO

Stupid is always late Good is always on time
excellent is always Early

Every man wonders what is the big surprise
that will forever close their eyes?

The more time you use the less you got
Time is a runner that never stops

No one knows where thoughts come from
not wise to except everyone's thoughts come
and go

Youth take time in life for periodic honest
introspection to focus your direction

I'm in terror but that's OK terror is a part of
life that people live through today

Take life slow you don't know when you'll go
or where you go you just know you go take
life slow

♫

Poetry has a ancestral spirit a poet must hear
it

Hidden fears breed hidden tears sometimes
too many beers

Now is new

Now Is Now
Now Is New
    It matter only what you do
        Something old or something new
       It's up to you♪
Now is New
Now is New
  The past is history
  The future a mystery
Now is New
Now is New
  Right this moment!
  You can do something new♪
Now is New
  Yesterday went away
   What you gonna do today?
    What you gonna do with now?
     What you gonna do with now?♪
      Because
Now is New
  It matter only what you do
  Something old or something new
Now is New♪
  Right this moment do something new
  Because a stagnated mind don't stagnated time♪
   Time just leaves it behind and move on to.....
Now is New Now is New Now is New
    Right this moment Do something new
      Now is New   Now is New

♫

I read many great spiritual books talked to
many wise spiritual
   Men yet I learned more about living a
spiritual life
          listening to the voice in me my
heartbeat and
                the wind

Maat or Ma'at was the ancient Egyptian concept of **truth, balance, order, harmony, law, morality, and justice**. "Maat was also personified as a goddess regulating the stars, seasons, and the actions of both mortals and the deities, who set the order of the universe from chaos at the moment of creation." ("Maat or ma'at was the Ancient Egyptian concept of truth ...")

Applying the principles of Maat, and honoring the laws/ideas of Maat, will bring balance and order to one's life.

Maat Seven Principles

Truth
Balance
Order
Harmony
Righteousness
Morality
Justice

♩

My Daily Prayer

42 Laws/Ideas of Maat

1. I honor virtue
2. I benefit with gratitude
3. I am peaceful
4. I respect the property of others
5. I affirm that all life is sacred
6. I give offerings that are genuine
7. I live in truth
8. I regard all altars with respect
9. I speak with sincerity
10. I consume only my fair share
11. I offer words of good intent
12. I relate in peace
13. I honor animals with reverence
14. I can be trusted
15. I care for the earth
16. I keep my own council
17. I speak positively of others
18. I remain in balance with my emotions
19. I am trustful in my relationships
20. I hold purity in high esteem
21. I spread joy
22. I do the best I can
23. I communicate with compassion
24. I listen to opposing opinions
25. I create harmony
26. I invoke laughter
27. I am open to love in various forms
28. I am forgiving
29. I am kind

30. I act respectfully
31. I am accepting
32. I follow my inner guidance
33. I converse with awareness
34. I do good
35. I give blessings
36. I keep the waters pure
37. I speak with good intent
38. I praise the Goddess and the God
39. I am humble
40. I achieve with integrity
41. I advance through my own abilities
42. I embrace the All

♩

About the Author

As a legendary poet, educator, and multi-dimensional artist, born in Houston Texas, and raised in Watts, CA. Amdepoet is also a founding member of the world-renowned Watts Prophets poetry group, recognized for first defining and developing the universal artform of what is called rap. The Watts Prophets' 1969 album *Black Voices: On the Streets in Watts* was heralded by *Rolling Stone* magazine for being one of the 40th most groundbreaking albums of all time. The Watts Prophets 1971 album *Rappin' Black in a White World* is documented as the first album to publish the word *rappin'* to define an art form in its title and composition.

Amdepoet first began his writing career at the critically acclaimed 1965 Watts Writers' Workshop. Throughout his prolific career, he has studied and collaborated with some of the world's most noted artists, including Don Cherry, Horace Tapscott, Billy Higgins, Bob Marley, Nina Simone, Quincy Jones, Richard Pryor, and Oscar Browne Jr.

In addition, Father Amde became ordained as an Ethiopian Orthodox Priest and studied under the tutelage of Archbishop Abuna Yesehaq of the Western Hemisphere, receiving the name Father Amdetzion, which means pillar of heaven. Amde was hosted by Pope Shenouda III of Alexandria to reside at his private home in Egypt. After the community struggled with the pronunciation of his name, Amdepoet asked that the people refer to him as Father Amde, which is still the name many friends, fans, and historical references use today. As Father Amde, he spearheaded the first gang truce with the first-known conception of the infamous Bloods and Crips Los Angeles street gangs. Father Amde later baptized the High Priestess of Soul Nina Simone, and presented a poem at his friend's funeral, the late-great reggae superstar Bob Marley.

Amdepoet continued to write and perform poetry across the globe with the Watts Prophets. He also kept family at his core, working and creating with the love of his life and wife of 58 years, Momma Shirley Hamilton. Father Amde's family, community, and world ties over the years have made him a rare jewel. With over 50 grandchildren and hundreds of great and great-great grandchildren, his legacy is ever evolving into future generations to come.

Recently, Amdepoet and Oshea Luja has spearheaded the return of the Watts Writers' Workshop "to provide an area of expression for those with no area of expression." He remains connected to his beloved community of Watts, most recently organizing and leading the charge to save the Mafundi building (the early hub for many soon-to-be legendary Los Angeles artists) in Watts, CA, influencing the city to nominate the site as a historical landmark to house

Watts's ebony history, culture, and tradition, and restore the historic creative programs that made the Watts Happening Cultural Center (Mafundi building) great.

For more about Amdepoet, visit:
www.WattsProphets.org.

♪